FamilyTime

Prepared and Published by the
Family Communication Committee
of the Million Dollar Round Table

Grady Nutt, Author

Graphic Design by Design Group 3, Inc., Chicago

*No other success
can compensate for
failure in the home.*

Section One

Wherein is discussed

The reason for this book
The rationale for its content
and suggestions
For making use of the suggestions . . .

This book is being prepared for families throughout the world.

It was written with 1976 in mind . . .

which is crucial
when you get *1776* in mind . . .

bicentennial
American history
200
Paul Revere
George Washington
independence
flags
make-your-own candles
trailblazing

and all that.

A. Dan Wilson

Hikers travel slower than jet pilots and see much more detail on the journey . . .

FamilyTime is an effort to get speeding families to slow down

and smell the roses
see the colors
feel the textures
taste the sweetness
(sometimes tartness)
of quality together-time.

Very-first-thing-to-notice: most families do not spend much time together uninterrupted by

          ballgames
          chores
          television
          meetings
          loud music
          quiet music;

most families do not spend much time together
          listening to each other;

most families do not spend much time together!

FamilyTime has one bull's eye (only one)
in the center of one target (only one):

FamilyTime has one bull's eye (only one)
in the center of one target (only one):

each family
would benefit from
a weekly time together
spent on and in
quality projects/events/times
that enrich
deepen
bring joy to
family living

Before reading further, please read that
italics part one more time...
(Pause while italics part is being re-read)
Thanks...

now, let's step lightly into the foyer of

THE FAMILY IN HISTORY

for a moment. . .

The family has been	a main cog in the wheel
	a prime color in the rainbow
	a capital letter in the sentence
	a captain of the team
	a motor on the boat

of the history of nations. . .	families settled farms and villages
	families created a thirst for independence
	families established laws
	families fought for freedom
	families explored and settled wilderness
	families built schools
	families built homes
	towns
	cities. . .
	families created nations.

It was as exciting to find a new way to dye
thread in 1776 as it is to develop a
transistor in 1976 . . .
and maybe just about as important.

A. Dun Wilson

Back then you had to grow your wheat
grind your flour
mix your ingredients
bake your loaf *yourself* . . .

TODAY,   a computerized bakery
         twists the airholes out
         thinslices and plasticbags it
         and delivers it
         to a store near you . . .

Bread makers at home are a modern
miracle!

A. Dan Wilson

All that to pay tribute to hard working
pioneer spirits . . .
    all that to remind us
    that no one else
    can do your family for you
    like the bakery can do your bread.
Bread without the bag gets dry . . .
    statistical information alone
    is like dry bread.
These items come from a study by the
Institute of Life Insurance
    and have
    a "fresh bread"
    purpose . . .

Item: "Divorce rates have doubled since the '50's."

Item: "There is a blurring of the sex roles and the traditional place of man and woman in the family."

Item: "There is a greatly reduced emphasis on the virtue of self-denial and self-sacrifice for the sake of the family."

Item: "Increasing numbers of people wish to preserve the institutions of family and marriage but want to change the rules dramatically."

Item: "There is a substantial erosion of the rituals of the family institution (such as family meals together, social times together)."

Item: You are probably not shocked by any of this . . .

It is the basic contention of **FamilyTime**
that the family
is an indispensable component
in personal and group development
and should be encouraged
enhanced
enlivened
with all the strength you can muster . . .
and you can muster a bunch of strength
right here in these pages.
The secret word (be ready!) is

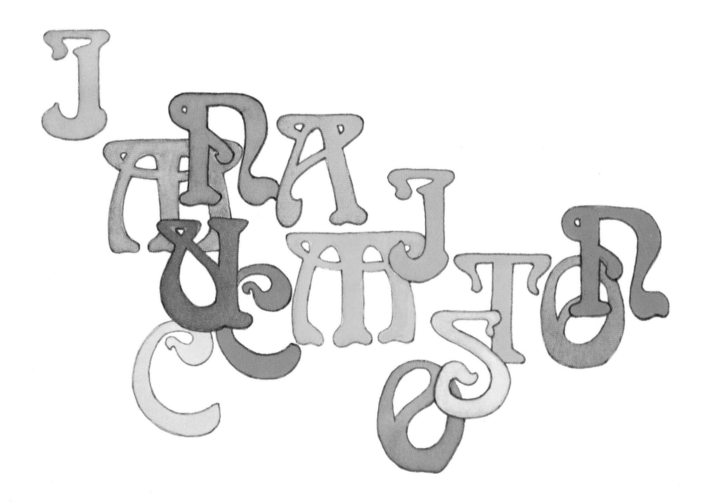

COMMUNICATION

COMMUNICATION

the most-said
least-well-done word
in our language.
No play will work in an athletic effort
No company will correlate efforts
No organization will function smoothly
No friendship will exist
without *communication*.
Communication is not just getting it *said*.
Communication is getting it *heard*.
Good family communication is a
two-way
three-way
four-way
more-way street.
Good communication must happen in the
family from many directions:
parent-to-parent/child-to-child
parent-to-child/child-to-parent
all of these are channels for free-
flow or the "hardened arteries"
that do damage to the family.
Bluntly...
this book was written
solely to help your family
talk with and to each other
constructively, wisely,
compassionately, well,
and *often*...even *regularly*.

COMMUNICATION

What is it?
Among other things it is
honest/straightforward talk
sensitive listening
touching
avoiding one another purposefully
loving living together...
It is hearing what was said
and
knowing what was meant...
It is the beautiful blend of
space and proximity
up-close and apart...
It is fair rules...
for parents and children alike...
It is sharing...
ideas
time
interests
things
concerns...
Ultimately, it is deep care and
love for each other
that gets said
that gets heard!

COMMUNICATION

How does it happen?
It happens when what I feel

about what you have done or said
gets to you in
     an honest form
     an honest atmosphere of love.
It happens when what you feel
about what I have done or said
gets to me in
     an honest form
     an honest atmosphere of love.
(It is as honest to say *I love you*
as it is to say
     I have a bone to pick with you . . .)

It happens when I unbottle feelings
                              information
                              concern
                              anger
                              fun . . .
     It happens in good form
          so
          very
          seldom
               in most families . . .

FamilyTime:

A Revolutionary Old Idea
which you hold
in your hand
     was written for the sake of people
     who love their families
          and their family time together . . .
     it is intended to stimulate families
     to spend a night each week
     (repeat)

to spend a night each week
     together
          talking
          playing
          sharing
     together
          confessing
          asking
          telling

     together!

There is no question that
a multitude of family styles
shapes
sizes
make-ups
structures

exist . . .
families directed
by only one parent . . .
families in every social
and economic level

it is to that diversity
that **FamilyTime** is dedicated . . .
with the hope/wish/prayer
that families put together
in different ways
may know each other better
may exercise their unique gifts
may grow in strength
and closeness

and may help our nations
throughout the world
to become one brotherhood
at peace at home
at peace next door
at peace . . .

everywhere!

Section Two

Wherein is found a series of activities/Family-
Times aimed at enabling families to play,
to talk, to share, to have fun together. . .
Consider spending a night at home with your
family each week. . . Here are some things to
do while you're together. . . You'll probably find
that FamilyTime is the best time of all . . .

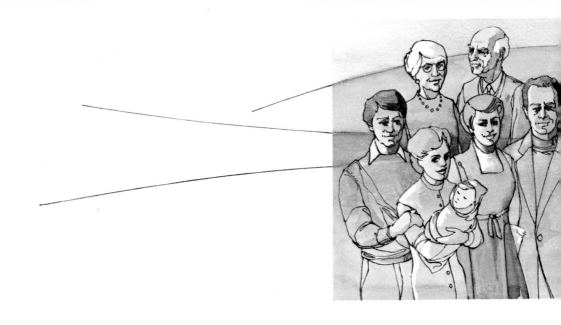

FamilyTimes   This is Section Two, the core and heart of **FamilyTime.** This book has been prepared for one purpose only: to encourage your family to try some time doing things you enjoy doing together. No activity in its own strength or ingenuity can bring solidarity and communication to your home; but people who want to relate to one another honestly can use some games and suggested activities as "the soil out of which good families grow best!"

Section Two has four parts. The first part is called "ShareTimes." These are activities that include some advance preparation and cooperation from most of the family members. They are aimed primarily at stimulating conversation from the family on various levels and around numerous topics.

The second part consists of "ActivityTimes." Here the emphasis is on things to *do* together. Suggestions are given to get you to play, laugh, and otherwise enjoy one another.

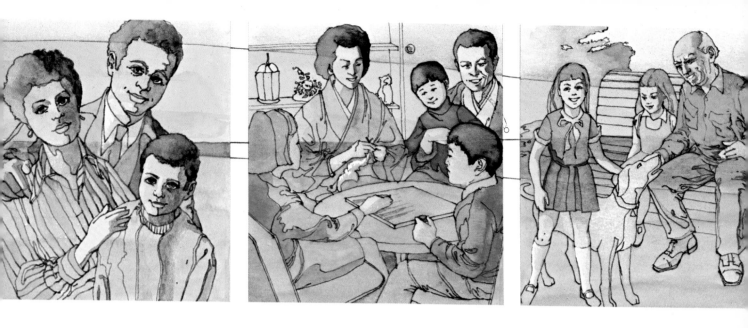

The third part is made up of "OutingTimes." These are suggestions of things the family might do away from the home. Included are some special family projects you might wish to consider.

The fourth part is called "Revolutionary Old Ideas." Here you will find discussion material based on basic moral values (integrity, loyalty, faith, patriotism, etc.). This section should give your family a chance to remember and discuss crucial principles that made many nations great.

In Section One we wave a flag and stand on our heads and shoot off rockets with red-white-blue glare and say: "This book is worth your time and valuable to your family!" We shout that; we "yell-'til-we're-hoarse" that!

In Section Three we give you an abbreviated map of the family showing the roses and possible landmines along the way. In Section Two we are saying: "Here is rain for your parched desert, snow for your ski slope, bass for your fishhook, a moon for your courting, and fun for your family."

This is worth your time.
This can help your family.
Come on in . . .
The water is fine!

A Family "How-To" Night

Purpose of the Evening and the Exercise: To use simple things that each family member needs to know how to do as a basis for spending an interesting evening at home together.

Preparations: Check through the list of things to be done with the family tonight to be sure you have the necessary items and tools to do these things together.

Parents should be together on what things can be done with the entire family. Some items ("changing a car tire") may be well ahead of your six- and four-year-old children!

The general basic assumption of this evening's activities is that there are many things children can learn from their parents that parents assume the children already know. Parents can learn many things from each other, and parents can learn from children.

Should be a fun night at home!

Procedures:

(1) Telephone
  A. Be sure everyone knows how to dial a number. Be sure everyone understands direct dialing, the cost of calls, how to place a credit card call (in case of emergency, to call when away from home) or collect call. Be sure everyone knows how to look up a number in the phone book. Be sure

everyone understands how the Yellow Pages are arranged. Give some brief directions, such as looking up a name or looking up a carpet cleaner.

B. Post emergency numbers carefully in a conspicuous place. Be certain everyone knows the family doctor's number, the fire, police, and ambulance number.

C. Give careful instructions on how to answer the phone, how to take messages. Be sure some kind of pen-and-pad arrangement is made for message-taking.

(2) Go over "how to write a check." Explain the procedures of banking. Explain savings accounts, interest, related matters. Plan to take the children to the bank to see how deposits and withdrawals are accomplished. Open savings accounts for each child, if possible.

(3) Go over the family budget. Explain income, outgo. Explain insurance. Help children establish their own budgets. Check up on them to be sure they are managing it well.

(4) Manners review. Take time to go over items like "which fork," "seating ladies," "May I be excused?" Touch on "chewing with your mouth open" and "talking with your mouth full." Remind each other in a fun way of shortcomings.

(5) How to operate the vacuum cleaner. Changing the vacuum bag. What to do with it.

(6) Operating other modern conveniences:
   A. Dishwasher
   B. Blender
   C. Power mower
   D. Stereo
   E. Electric can opener/knife/ice crusher

(7) Operate the sewing machine. Get Dad to sew a bit, run some stitches, make a seam.

(8) Change a car tire or a bike tire.

(9) Show how to use the bathroom plunger ("plumber's friend") in the event of a stopped drain. Know where to shut off the main water supply.

(10) Change a fuse. Show how to re-activate a circuit breaker in the event it trips.

(11) Show how to set the table properly.

(12) Give a lesson in cookie-baking.

(13) Give lessons in cooking simple things: toast, scrambled eggs, soups, bacon.

(14) Dad teaches Mom how to measure and saw wood, hammer, figure angles, run a power drill.

(15) Show how to change a light switch. Be sure to show where to cut off the power supply.

(16) Spend some time using a new calculator, the new electronic variety. They will be increasingly inexpensive and available to homes, offices and schools.

(17) Give a lesson in using the oven. Know how to shut off the main gas supply.

(18) Devise a plan for evacuation of the entire family in case of fire. Secure pamphlets from your fire department giving basic information on evacuation and then add your own plans tailored to your house and your family needs. Go through the fire drill numerous times: plan surprise drills with some regularity to be certain the plan is remembered and executed properly.

(19) Above all, *emphasize safety.* Leave nothing to chance. Be certain that adults who have been using the power mower for years know the basic rules about starting and running it.

Purpose: The aim is *affirmation.* Each member of the family will be encouraged to share with every other family member a significant positive feeling—hopefully *many* such feelings. The characters of the *Peanuts* cartoon strip are suggested here as a starting point; however, your family can get into the swing of the evening using any other comic strip or even the characters of a favorite television program (*Sesame Street* with very young children, *All in the Family* with older children).

Preparation: Collect Sunday and/or daily comic strips. You may find in a news-stand or a bookstore some paperback copies of the *Peanuts* cartoons. You may also wish to collect posters, shirts, drinking glasses, stationery, cards, etc. bearing the *Peanuts* images to use during the evening. *Obviously, if you are using another favorite comic strip, you will need to make necessary changes.*

Make special plans to use some of the materials as table decorations. You may drink out of *Peanuts* glasses, use *Peanuts* napkins, *Peanuts* placecards. Any of these can be homemade using a little Elmer's Glue and cut-outs from the cartoon strips you are using.

Have available several sheets of plain white paper, even the children's notebook paper, along with pencils or pens, maybe even crayons for the smaller children.

Be sure to have a good store of family favorite snacks on hand (popcorn, soft drinks, cake, homemade ice cream). Depending on your family, you might want to go really "Peanutty" and have only snacks that could be made from some derivative of peanuts: peanut butter and jelly finger sandwiches, dry roasted peanuts, peanut butter milkshakes, etc.

Family Night with the Comics

Procedure: (1) Ask each member of the family to pick the comic character with whom he most identifies. In other words, "Which *Peanuts* character reminds you of yourself?" Write the name of the character (Charlie Brown, Linus, Snoopy, Lucy) on your paper.

Now. . .each person should share with the rest of the family the character picked and why that particular character was chosen.

Then. . .take a few minutes and write down on your paper all the things you really like about the character you chose. ("I chose Lucy, and I like these things about Lucy. . .")

(With smaller children, you may wish to make cut-outs of the characters and let the children pick from the pile of characters the one they feel most strongly about. It would be a good idea to cut out more than one of each character since more than one family member may identify with the same character.)

Share with the rest of the family the things you have written down about your character.

(2) On your paper list the names of each of the other family members. By each family member's name put the name of the character he or she most reminds you of.

Now. . .take one member at a time in the family (for instance, start with Mom) and let each member tell which character he/she chose to represent that person and why.

Then. . .go back around the circle and let each family member tell all the things he likes, admires, loves about the character he chose for that person. ("I picked Snoopy for Sarah. These are the things I like most about Snoopy. . .")

(3) Finally, take your paper and list each member of the family. Beneath each family member's name list all the things you genuinely love and admire about that person.

Go around the circle again, one person at a time, and let each tell the family member "in the hot seat" what things he/she loves most about that person.

Bonus Idea: Use the old "spin-the-bottle" game as a family affirmation idea. Sit in a circle (on the floor, around a table) and spin a soft drink bottle. The one who spins the bottle must make an affirming and positive statement about the family member who gets "pointed" by the bottle. This can go on for some time and should bring some great spontaneous thoughts about one another.

Suggestion: Do not say *to the family,* "I love the way Dad . . ." Instead, say *to Dad:* "I love the way you . . ."

Conclusion: Go around the family one more time and share highlights, surprises, discoveries, good feelings with each other. What has the evening meant to *you?*

**A Family
Service Project**

Purpose: To discover the joy of doing something for someone else without any thought of reward or recognition. To experience the joy of doing such a thing together, as a family.

Preparations: Several days ahead, the family should discuss the idea of a "family service project." There are many things that could be done. Consider them carefully, then choose one which seems best to suit the resources and time of the family.

Procedure: This is a list of several suggested activities for a "FamilyTime"...

(A) Do the fall leaf-raking or regular lawnmowing for an elderly neighbor who would have great difficulty doing it alone or might have to hire it done.

(B) Become a support family to a child in an orphanage or children's home. Arrange to have him or her in your home regularly, or perhaps provide spending money and some special things like clothing, records.

(C) Accept an ecology project. Check with city or other government authorities and agree to clean up the bank of a creek or stream, de-litter a park area, or other project they might suggest to you.

(D) Have a family-cookie-baking night and send them to a serviceman or college student from the neighborhood.

(E) Provide transportation to the store, to church, to doctor's appointments, etc. for a family or person in the neighborhood.

Where the activity can be done with secrecy, the family will reap an additional reward of doing something helpful that can be a surprise to the receiver.

Numerous activities
can be discovered
by the family that wants
to do a special deed
"just for the love of helping."

Purpose: To use the story of a movie or television program as the input for a significant family discussion. To use these media as more than just entertainment. . .

Preparation: Parents should be on the alert for a movie or television program that deals with a crucial issue or raises some helpful questions. Make meal and time allotments to permit the entire family to do this project together.

The movie or television show may be one the parents or children may have seen already and know to be the kind of material that will lend itself to a good Family-Time discussion. If any or all of the family have seen the program, then some discussion area could be agreed upon in advance. Also, some advance suggestions might be made to the members of the family as to what to look for in the program or show that will form the basis of the discussion later.

Procedure: For a television show or movie at home, you may wish to follow the program immediately with a time of conversation and discussion. For a movie, you may wish to see it one night and discuss it the next night or at a time close to the viewing.

TIME

DISCUSSION

You may own a projector, or can borrow one that will allow you to use movies from your public library. This would allow you considerable flexibility in making your discussion time fit your family schedule.

You will sometimes find a program that "sneaks up on you" and presents you with a beautiful "teachable moment." (See page 80 in Section Three.) You may just wish to turn off the set or, driving home from the movie, stop for a dish of ice cream and discuss the implications of what you have just seen as a family.

Brainstorm: A new technology is going to make video cassette taping of programs for family use available to families in the future. This is a wonderful way to capture meaningful programs for later viewing with the entire family. Parents could catch a late show on television, tape it with this kind of discussion in mind, and show it even two or three years later when the child or children have attained sufficient maturity and age-level to be able to deal with the matter wisely. It will also be possible at that time to lease, borrow, or buy special tapes for home viewing to be used in some careful program of family growth and dialogue.

Family Awards Night

Purpose: Basically this is a gag night, aimed at real fun, family-style, based on calling attention to family "achievements" with awards of a gag nature. This should be a real *laugh-in* kind of night!

Preparation:

1. Two or three days ahead of time, draw a name of one family member from a bowl or hat. That family member gets to suggest the menu for dinner...*anything* he or she wants to propose. It may even involve going out to a favorite food place, then coming home for the awards.

2. Each family member is to dream up at least one award for each of the other members. The award may be made from almost anything:

    A soap carving
    Cans soldered or glued together
    An old key with a ribbon on it
    Odd-shaped sticks standing in clay

3. A second award for each member, from each member, should be of a serious nature. These should be the last ones given.

Procedure: Take one family member at a time and place that person in the "seat of honor." Let each other member of the family present his "award" to the member-of-the-moment. (Save the serious awards 'til last.)

All the gag gifts and awards having been presented, go around with the more serious awards. Play up the good virtues of helpfulness, thoughtfulness, achievement, promptness, growth, mature decisions, etc. These awards can be equally unique in their construction, using handwork, baking, etc.

A great deal of mutual affirmation should result from this phase of the evening. It should be a time of great gratitude for the importance of each member of the family.

Variations: At any time, a special awards night could be declared. Dad gets a promotion or a new job: each member of the family dreams up a special award for him. Mom gets elected to a PTA office: she is the receiver of family awards. Give special certificates, plaques, mementos to the brand new teen-ager on his thirteenth birthday. Sally Sue gets her driver's license: special awards night could include presentation of a first aid kit, speedway permit, etc.

It is a great time and a great way to have family fun!!

**A Musical Night
To Remember**

Purpose: To learn to appreciate music that may be liked in different ways for different reasons by different family members. Music can be inspirational, fun, or both.

Preparation: Collect many different kinds of "rhythm band" instruments—paper and comb, spoons and pans, "kazoo's," harmonica, ukulele, guitar, or any other music-makers that can be dreamed up. Also, collect favorite albums and tapes for listening. You may also wish to secure sheet music for singing along with the piano or guitar. There are several collections of hit songs published with some regularity; any music store would likely have some music of this kind.

Procedure: After dinner, and more particularly after dinner *dishes* are done, gather together in the family room or living room (or in the carport if you have fragile glassware!) with all the musical instruments, records, tapes and sheet music

you have assembled. Begin with the performance of several favorite classics—*Old MacDonald Had a Farm, Turkey in the Straw,* etc.—played on the rhythm instruments.

Younger children will especially enjoy making music on different instruments.

Next, alternate listening to music on recordings with singing along with the piano or guitar. Each family member should get to play several selections that he or she especially enjoys—parents should feature some of their "old timey favorites," and the children should play everything from nursery-rhyme tunes to hard rock.

Try to hear each other's choices and appreciate where each member of the family draws his pleasure in music. Parents then might take this as a family principle and encourage a variety of music in the family all the time during the day when the radio is on or when recordings are being played.

Family Traditions   *Purpose:* To look at habits and activities that have developed in the family that bring a sense of history and joy together for us. To "walk in familiar and comfortable moments together" with thanksgiving and warm memories.

Preparation: Consider how many "traditional" things you do as a family and list them. Try to plan the evening meal around one particular tradition—such as, hamburgers on the charcoal grill every Saturday night. Do your traditional superb job of the evening menu to set the pace for the FamilyTime discussion.

Gather several reminders of the family traditions. If the family gathers on Sunday afternoon to watch professional football on television, perhaps you might have a football in the grouping. Certain ornaments are always in the Christmas tree box— have one or two of them on hand. Mom always has cookies and milk with the children when they come home from school—have a tray with cookies and milk available.

Procedure: Give each person a piece of paper and a pencil. Have each person quietly list all the "traditional" things the family does that bring joy to him or her.

Compare the lists after they are made and eliminate duplications. Now, go down the list one tradition at a time and see how the tradition developed in the family. Point out some of the "goofy" things that have happened in the process of doing these pleasant things.

(One family, for example, has a tradition of wrapping the birthday presents for each member of the family in strange and sometimes hilarious wrappings: comics, grocery sacks, seventeen black plastic trash can liners, toilet tissue, rags.)

Have the parents tell about traditions in their childhood that brought them security and a sense of belonging. Are there any traditions they miss now? Are there any that have carried over into their present family situation? Do some mean more than others? If so, why?

One helpful suggestion might be to decide on some traditional things you'd like to do as a family, such as: dinner "anywhere-you-choose" with the family on your birthday; selecting a live Christmas tree each year which you plant after Christmas, etc. Plan some traditions that can grow in your family!

Does the tradition of a
regular "FamilyTime"
appeal to everyone?
How has it helped?
What have we learned
about each other,
about family,
for having taken
this time together?

Purpose: To allow parents and other family members who have had experiences in school or in school-like settings to remember and share lessons learned from very special people in their lives, their teachers! The ultimate goal of this Family-Time is to sharpen awareness of the good influence on us by others and our chance to influence others for good.

Preparation: Make the meal time fun with ordinary, school-type food. Make sandwiches and put them in brown paper sacks. Make each person's lunch bag different than the others; encourage swapping of "this apple" for "those cookies," etc. Be sure to blow the bag up and pop it after you are through!

Placecards could be made from black construction paper and written on with chalk. During the meal the family cut-up could be given a dunce cap and made to wear it for the balance of the meal. Mom and Dad could set the tone for a "silly" evening by coming to the table dressed like children, with painted-on freckles, slicked-down hair, short pants, pigtails, etc.

A fun thing around the table would be a *spelling bee*, with one of the children selecting the words to be spelled. Each person could be given five cookies and one cookie would be forfeited for each word missed. One could be eaten for each word spelled correctly. Of course, children would get the tough words (like *cat, dog* and *pig*) while the parents and older brothers and sisters would get the easy words (like *Constantinople, restaurant,* and *Mississippi.*)

Procedure: Following dinner, gather in the living room or family room. Begin with the parents and let them each tell of fun things he or she did in early school days (frog in a girl's lunch pail, sending a note to a boy telling him of your "great undying love" and signing another girl's name.) Encourage others in the family of all ages to tell similar fun things they did in school.

Next, spend some time telling about things you did in school that you got punished for in some way. This, as the first part, should be begun by parents. Confess whatever you can stand to be reminded of through the years!

Finally, dwell on some of the teachers along the way who have had special influence on your life. Lead the family to discuss these questions together:

    (1) What were their outstanding characteristics as teachers?
    (2) Did they treat all students fairly?
    (3) Did they make learning a joy?
    (4) What impressed you most about each teacher?
    (5) Is there any trait of your favorite teacher that you would like to have in your own life?

Purpose: To deal with our basic values as members of the family. How do I determine values? What is valuable to me? What do I value in others? **Values**

Preparation: Dinner should be served with a motif of a desert island, using Robinson Crusoe-type decorations or placecards. The children could make a small desert island scene on cardboard to place in the center of the table. Following the meal, some member of the family who has read *Robinson Crusoe* or perhaps the *Swiss Family Robinson* could tell that story around the table, emphasizing the need to be resourceful and the very real awareness of most of the things we could do without.

Procedure: Following dinner, during which time the desert island setting has been established, the family gathers in the family room. Talk briefly about the story of the marooned shipwreck victim or victims; ask what things were the most valuable to these people on their island. (Matches, wood, some tools, etc.)

Now—ask each person in the family to go to his or her room for fifteen minutes with this one question: "If you knew a flood, tornado, or fire were about to destroy your home and all your possessions, what would you grab up to take out with you? What would you try to save from destruction?"

After fifteen minutes, reassemble the family. Have each person bring back with him or her what he values most of all his possessions.

One person at a time, tell why you picked what you brought with you. Why is it valuable to you?

Conclusion: How many things did the family learn it could do without? Did the things considered "valuable" have very high replacement costs?

Discuss the *value* of
  A good mind
  A healthy body
  Good friends
  Ingenuity and imagination.

Discuss this statement: "There are people who know the cost of everything and the value of nothing!"

In this same section on page 61 you will find a discussion and content portion called "Revolutionary Old Ideas." In the spirit of this FamilyTime, you may wish to use some of the suggested topics and materials for this particular treatment on basic values.

Decision Making

Purpose: To discuss as a family the process by which decisions are made in the family. There should be a desire to deal not only with how decisions are made and by whom, but also with how inadequate processes can be altered for the benefit of the entire group.

Preparation: As a different mealtime activity, let the youngest member of the family (if old enough for this!) decide where every other member of the family shall sit for dinner tonight. This also means that this child gets to choose his or her own spot at the table and everyone else has to sit where he or she is told to sit.

Before the FamilyTime discussion, it would be very helpful for the parents to talk with one another about various aspects of decision-making in the family. In Harry Truman's words, "where does the buck stop" in your family? Are you prepared as parents to deal with the possible need for changes in your way of deciding the broad range of things that the family deals with every day? Do you recognize any areas in the family decision-making process that need to be restructured?

Procedure: Provide some paper and a pencil for each member of the family. Younger children could have their "lists" made for them by parents or older brothers and sisters.

List first the areas for each family member where he or she has total control over the decisions in his life. Dad might list such things as where he will work, accepting or refusing promotions and job changes, what to wear to work, what his hobbies will be, etc. Mom might list how to have her hair styled, what clothes to buy, what to cook for dinner, etc. A child might list how to decorate his or her room, how long to wear his hair, what clothes to wear to school, who his or her friends will be, whether or not to play a school sport this year.

Next list the things where you have little or no decision-making freedom or power. Do you feel comfortable about these? Would you like to see any changes?

Finally, what decisions could the family be making together in a better way? Discuss things like money matters, vacation trips, where to spend the holidays, who gets to use the family car and under what circumstances, etc.

Make some suggestions about how you might alter any ways you are now handling such matters, try some new guidelines for several weeks, then have another night with the family to evaluate and sharpen your decisions.

Some families find that the idea of a *family council* is a very good forum for discussing major and even minor decisions.

Example: Marvin is now seventeen and feels that the rules about car privileges and curfews should be updated. He talks with Mom about it after school one day, and she feels it is a matter for the family council. Marvin's feelings are heard, parents' attitudes are aired, others in the family are heard from, and a decision is reached together. Marvin has been part of the decision to handle matters in this fashion, and he is agreeable to discuss it with the entire family and reach a conclusion that all participate in equally.

Nifty Idea: Some night serve a beef casserole or meat loaf. Call it "Beef Session Special." Then let the family night take the form of family "beefs" about various things. Primary objective: to allow the family to have some forum where they are encouraged to speak their minds about various facets of the family situation. Suggestions taken seriously can be exceptionally rewarding.

**Favorite Meal Night
(or, Favorite Menu Time)**

This could be a part of the regular FamilyTime each week. Each member of the family in turn should get to request the menu for a particular meal. It could also be varied so that another night of the week could be designated as *Family Menu Time.*

There might even be a "menu suggestion box" or special note pad made available so family members could drop in a note at any time requesting a favorite dish or full meal. As magazines are being read, menu suggestions with "delicious pictures" could be clipped and made available to the chief cook.

How about a "recipe rating time?" The usual chef would submit the recipe box to the family for evaluation. Super meals, the kind you'd even crave as leftovers, would get a *10,* recipes getting only a *1* get burned in the charcoal grill next time we do hamburgers.

Don't overlook "out-to-eat-nights." The family might decide that one night each month—maybe the second Thursday—would be restaurant night. Each family member could decide the place to eat so all would have a turn. Keep a record of who-picked-what-place-when for future reference.

Note Night

Most families do not do well at keeping in touch with other family members and close family friends. Try *Note Night!*

Tonight have adequate paper (stationery, notebook stock) available for each family member. Make a list together following dinner; name family members and friends who will be included in the notes we write.

Gather around a table if possible. Have adequate snacks and drinks available. One at a time mention the various people you have determined to "note" this time. As each person or family is mentioned, let each member of the family write a brief note. Have fun with it. Mention silly and fun things as well as expressing genuine concerns for their welfare. When each person has written his or her note, seal them in an envelope, address it for mailing, and continue to the next person or family listed.

Imagine being on the other end of that mailing! Great fun to hear from everyone in your family.

This would also be a great October or November FamilyTime to prepare Christmas cards from your family.

Few, if any, modern inventions have as much to offer family communication as the cassette tape recorder. Its compact and convenient format is a boon to persons who have learned to use it well. For keeping up with your greater family and friends, this is a jewel! Some possible uses:

(1) *Tape letters:* Use tapes as a way to talk with grandparents, married children, college students away from home, military personnel, or just "dear friends."

(2) *Record special FamilyTimes:* You might be having a FamilyTime when you remember family history, special ancestors, school days, religious heritage, family tree information, or other such matters. Set your recorder in the center of the group and record the conversation for future reference and memory.

(3) *Crucial family discussions:* Record those "once-in-a-lifetime" talks with your children. One father recorded the conversations he had with his two sons about intimate sexual information. He secured the permission of the boys to do the recording, promised never to let anyone outside the family hear the tapes, and plans to give each son a tape with those conversations in full *as a wedding gift!*

(4) *Vacations and trips:* On vacation and family trips keep your recorder handy for recording impressions of things you have seen, people you have visited and impressions of your time together. These tapes would make a terrific background for family movies, slides or album prints of the trip when they are viewed later.

(5) *Birthdays:* On each child's birthday interview him or her briefly about "where he is in his life at the moment." Record feelings, memories, fun things that are happening at the moment and other valuable information. Continue the tape each birthday for each child; you now have a reservoir of memories that your family will always cherish.

(6) *Telephone taping:* For a modest price (under $10.00) you can purchase a telephone jack that will let you record your telephone conversations with anyone at any time. For older family members you seldom get to see, a phone visit is most meaningful. Record these conversations as part of your family storehouse of information—with everyone's permission, of course.

(7) *Travel books:* Read favorite children's stories into a tape recorder; then take the books and tapes with you when you travel by car. This is a great way for children to pass the time on a trip, listening to Dad read a favorite story while they look at the book with its pictures. This is also a great idea for those rainy or messy days when the children can't play outdoors. Just turn on your tapes and turn on your children!

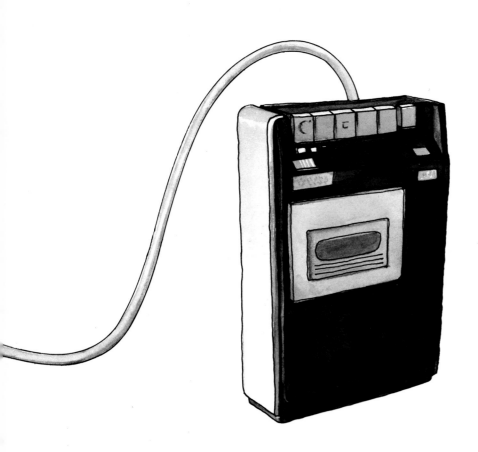

Here's a fun time together—*puzzles*. Smaller children usually have two or three puzzles they enjoy working many times. Encourage them to get their puzzles out so all the family can do the puzzles together.

For the older family members, purchase one of the "seven-zillion-tiny-hard-to-match-pieces" kind of puzzles with a picture on the outside of the box. To make it a truly tough time, don't look at the picture on the box.

Organize the pieces by color, grouping them in neat rows or clusters. Then start out with the straight-edged pieces and try to construct your borders. Fill it in as quickly as you can. You may want this to be your vacation week instead of just an evening at home together. Your family should be pretty strong to take the frustration certain puzzles can create! It may even help you figure out why some families are so hard to figure out or fit together!

An interesting suggestion with especially beautiful or difficult puzzles: glue them together on a sheet of plywood and frame them for the walls of the family room, a child's room or the garage!!

How about *Riddle Night?* Nearly everyone loves a good riddle. It could be a great FamilyTime to use riddles as the basis for the evening together.

You could start the dinner with a riddle menu. Describe the various items for the meal using riddles: for example—"They're a snap to fix." (Green beans.) Every item has to be guessed before the meal is served.

Secure books of riddles from your library. You might also wish to purchase two or three such books at a bookstore. Give each person a book (each one different from the others) and allow about fifteen minutes for a search through the book. Mark with strips of paper the riddles you wish to use on the family.

Go around the circle several times allowing each person to try to stump the family with his riddle choices.

The world's weirdest riddle: "Why do they paint firetrucks red?"

Answer: Three times four is twelve; there are twelve inches in a ruler, Queen Mary was a ruler; Queen Mary was a ship; ships sail on the sea; the sea has fish; fish have fins; the Fins fought the Russians; the Russians are red; Reds are always Russian; so are firetrucks; that's why they paint them red. Phew . . .

Game Night One "all-time" favorite family activity is the game. It is entirely possible that the first game ever played was played by a family group after a busy day at home in a cozy cave!

Use standard games with boards and other special helps: *Monopoly, Sorry, Backgammon, Parcheesi*, chess, etc.

Use card games: bridge, canasta, hearts, "go-fishing," *Rook, Old Maid*, etc. Remember that children also enjoy mazes as a game.

You can have an active game night with pool, bumper pool, ping-pong, darts or skittles. In good weather you could have a tennis night or an evening playing croquet, *Jarts*, badminton or miniature golf.

Continue to broaden your knowledge and supply of good family games. You might even have every member of the family give a special game to the entire family for Christmas. Use them regularly as "FamilyTimes."

And remember, *the family that plays together . . . loves to!*

Usually individuals keep diaries, but a family could do it, too. Find a method that suits your family best, but try in some way to capitalize on "feelings of that moment" that you will always want to remember.

A suggestion: on each family member's birthday, have him or her write in a family diary his reflections on the past year, memories of the day, gifts received, dreams dreamed and hopes hoped.

As each child grows up and leaves home, he or she could be given a typed or Xeroxed copy of the entire diary as a reminder of the good times together. It would be a marvelous thing to read at Thanksgiving or other special holiday time.

Slide/Movie/ Scrapbook/Album Night

All these forms are similar because they allow the family to record and later remember special moments together. Occasionally set up the projector or get out the scrapbook and albums and enjoy reminiscing together!

One very good FamilyTime would be to start a family scrapbook, if you do not already have one. Allow members of the family to include whatever they wish in order to have all the family well represented. Could even be a modest, in-house brag-book!

A super scrapbook can be made from an old wallpaper sample book. Check with a hardware or wallpaper store and get on their list of those who might wish to claim discontinued or outdated sample books.

With the endless variations you can create many reservoirs of good family memories. Take good pictures with still or motion cameras, show them or paste them up, and then get them out for some outstanding fun together.

Comedy Album Night

Some of the wittiest and funniest people alive have albums and tapes of their routines available. Most people who have any kind of sound system have some good comedy albums in their collection. Why not have a night when you play such favorite albums for each other? Some of the albums are ones you listened to several times two or three years ago and would enjoy hearing again.

Special Television Programs

Television can be the great blessing to the family or its great curse. It has probably robbed the family of conversation more than any single factor in history; but, it has often been the source of great strength and vitality for the family.

Seeing the first moonwalk, catching a presidential inauguration, seeing the Olympics from Munich as they occur, or watching a classic movie or play can make any problems created by television seem almost worth it all.

Pick programs that might give the family some helpful insight, some light entertainment, some touch with history, and then use the program as fodder for later conversation, maybe right after the program. Plan how you use television and it can be your good friend!

Walt Disney alone was worth the invention of moving pictures! His touch with fantasy and imagination is a rare and precious gift to the family. His commitment to decent and entertaining pictures has reaped its rightful reward: our trust and thanks as American families.

He is not alone. Sheer genius hits the silver screen night after night. However, as we are all aware, much of the film shot to show is wasted!

Plan a FamilyTime with your flock and see a genuinely helpful and entertaining family-oriented film. Use the story and thoughts conveyed as the basis for your family to discuss and evaluate some of your own living together. You might see the film one night, after a quick round of fast-service hamburgers, and discuss it the following night. You might also come right home and spend some time around cake and milk talking it over.

It is a splendid way to teach your children how to evaluate and show mature judgment in selecting and viewing films. It also helps to teach them that everything you see on the screen is not to be believed in the everyday world!

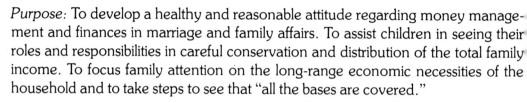

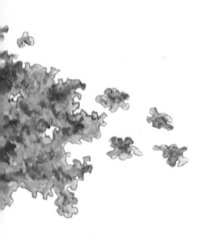

Financial FamilyTime

Purpose: To develop a healthy and reasonable attitude regarding money management and finances in marriage and family affairs. To assist children in seeing their roles and responsibilities in careful conservation and distribution of the total family income. To focus family attention on the long-range economic necessities of the household and to take steps to see that "all the bases are covered."

Preparation:

A. Some basic principles for family financial strength:

1. Wives and children should feel a part of family financial affairs.

2. Money and its "buy-products" can never substitute for love, affection and attention of caring parents.

3. Money should never be used as either bribe, reward or punishment.

4. Good family money management will help children develop a sound value system, clarify priorities. It will help teach a child to choose well in the general area of *all* his desires and needs, present and future.

5. Parents should encourage independent earning of income.

6. A child should learn to manage money under good supervision. He can learn early in life about basic documents, terms, institutions and procedures of family financial affairs. It will help him develop a solid awareness of his own potential for productivity.

7. Money management should take precedence in the family over money productivity: in other words, managing what you have may be a far greater trait to develop than the ability to acquire more and more funds.

8. Develop and *consistently live by* a sound family budget! Spend only what you have and borrow only when you must!

B. Some things to do:

1. Familiarize the entire family with the essential things they should know about family economics.

2. Summarize from tax records or bank statements the basic family expenditures; categorize by percentages (21% for housing, 17% for automobiles, etc.). Show and know where the money goes!

3. Gather together the basic family financial documents: wills, deeds, trusts, insurance papers, financial statements, etc.

4. Become familiar with Social Security and retirement benefits: share with your spouse any information you have on savings, life insurance investment programs, stock portfolios, land and properties owned, etc.

Procedure: Several suggestions for discussions of your family's finances are provided here. Based on principles already suggested, these general areas are the core of any successful money management going on in family life. There are three categories: general family financial picture, allowances and estate planning.

A. General Family Financial Picture

With as much openness as you feel appropriate, explain where the family income is derived. Be sure that all members old enough to understand can see the portions of income that go for taxes, social security, and other "withholdings."

It can be a good learning experience to discuss the family expenditures and obligations. You might show the family budget to everyone, and be sure that each one understands what percentage of the total pie is cut for each item. If no actual budget exists, the family would do well to spend one evening together arriving at a workable budget.

B. Allowances

It is generally recommended that each child should have an allowance which should start an an early age. It is considered a good practice that as soon as a child is old enough to give valid input, he or she should be included in the decisions relating to the allowance.

Most advisors feel that the allowance should not relate to the child's behavior. For example, they would recommend against withholding the allowance for poor grades in school or for staying out fifteen minutes past curfew.

It is sometimes a good learning experience to allow them to commit a short-term economic disaster that may well make him or her "long-term" wise about money.

When possible, start checking and savings accounts for each child. Let wise and confident use of allowance money be a valuable tool for teaching your child to make lifelong good decisions about his or her resources.

Some Additional Suggestions: Discuss the seriousness of paying an obligation on time as agreed. This is a part of basic integrity in business dealings.

Teach the children the value of saving *for* something. For example, show the value in saving for and planning for a specific project, a special purchase or a trip that will have lasting worth and merit for the child. One idea is for the parents to pledge a portion of the total objective if the child will save the rest.

Above all, you are encouraged to try to find a way to teach your child the joy of work. To work because you want to work is considered by many to be a rare thing in our day.

C. "Contingency" Time—A Time for Family Estate Planning

Young children will not likely be concerned with this area of family finance. However, couples will do well to acquaint one another and the older children with the basics of long-term planning for financial security—to spend time getting basic information on such matters clearly in focus so that in the event of a death or other untimely "contingency," good decisions may be made and all necessary papers and materials will be readily accessible.

Neither death nor disability run on a time schedule—and retirement time seems so often to catch a person unprepared financially. We don't plan to fail in providing for these contingencies in life, but all too often we fail to plan.

Planners strongly recommend establishing a *"Contingency Time"*—a special day set aside each year to discuss the problems that a catastrophe might bring. Establish a day that won't be forgotten—whatever day appeals to you.

Many widows and children can attest to the fact that a few hours of thoughtful family planning each year could have saved them endless hours—yes, even years—of confusion, heartache and fear. (See Bibliography—*The Widow*, by Lynn Caine).

Make *Contingency Time* a time to discuss the importance of responsible management of funds and properties. Take time to work with your advisors in preparing wills, and re-evaluate your plans each year in the light of changing circumstances. Go over your insurance program to make sure everyone understands how it works. . .and why it works. Share any information you can about investments in stocks, bonds, properties or other forms of basic security.

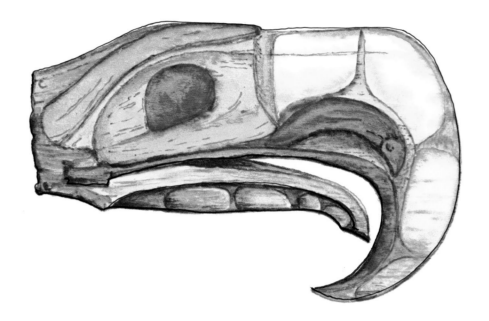

Zoo Day: Few things are more fun than a day at the zoo with children. Be sure to take your camera for snapshots or movies of the children being fascinated and amazed at the animals. It would be fun to have the children imitate animals at the various stops and photograph them with the animals in the background.

"Who does that remind you of?" It is fun to name the animals for the people they remind you of—Aunt Rachel, Weird Harold, or famous characters in the news or from history.

Museums: Museums are full of all kinds of good stuff for families. You can see "how it used to be," mummies, old cars, trains, farm tools, Indian villages and gadgets of every sort. Spend a day at a specialty museum, like one on air travel or maybe one on famous race horses.

Train ride: Too few people get to (or want to) ride trains in the modern age. Occasionally you will see advertised a special train trip (to the state capitol, to a ball game). One rail line recently closed out its passenger service on a traditionally vital route; they had a "last chance to ride" trip, and many families got to go together not just for the *last* ride, but some for the *first* time.

OutingTimes & Projects (cont.)

City Bus Trip: Suburban families in most cities do not take advantage of public transportation; in fact, most public transportation suffers in revenue because families insist on "doing it themselves." So, try a family bus trip.

Christmas holidays are approaching for you; put the entire family on a bus and go to town to do your shopping. You want to see a museum or attend a special matinee of a ballet or movie—take the bus together.

Plan a bus tour around the city one Saturday. Go from point A to point B, and do your thing there. Then bus to point C for your activity there; and so on until you have toured the city for part of the day. "Leave the driving to someone else" and just enjoy the day together!

Family Wildcard Ticket Book: One family gives the children "wildcard ticket books" on their birthdays. The book contains "tickets" such as: "This ticket entitles _____ to one day at the zoo with his/her parents." Children cash them in any time before next birthday for ball games, ice cream cones, pizza, movies, etc.

Sports Activities: Attend ball games, tennis matches, parachute jumps, the Indianapolis 500 or the Kentucky Derby! Go out to sports events as a family. This is generally an "everybody kind of thing." Take a thermos of hot chocolate or some cold drink (depending on the weather) along with the appropriate snacks, and you have a great afternoon or evening together.

Concerts / Plays / Ballet Performances: Along with visits to museums and other cultural enrichment possibilities, be sure to keep uppermost the opportunity to attend plays, concerts by local and touring symphonies, ballet performances, the opera and featured entertainment of a classical nature. You will do your family lasting good to introduce and involve them in the magnificent variety of the arts.

Be sure to read up on the programs you are to attend so you can do some pre-concert input for the family. Each member of the family will tend to enjoy the presentation more if he or she more fully understands what will be seen and heard.

State and National Parks: Most families are located fairly close to one or more state or national parks. Make use of these public facilities for camping, hiking, picnicking, nature study and other enjoyable outdoor activities. Don't overlook the "green grass" on *your* side of the fence!

Camping: Very likely, camping is the fastest growing family sport / activity in the nation. It takes every shape and form. People backpack, canoe, roll in a recreational vehicle, put up or simply open-after-parking the big travelling trailers. Families who do it regularly are borderline fanatics about family unity and the close feelings derived from spending quieter and deeper time together. There is some form of camping within the financial reach and territorial boundaries of nearly every family. Try it . . . you'll probably like it!

Fishing: From the biggest wigglin' worm to the $12.95-guaranteed-to-get-bass-bright-red-and-black-and-chrome-latest-plug-out, people love fishing. Families are great fishing buddies. Creeks, lakes, ponds are near most of us. No one is born knowing how to do it; everyone has to learn. If parents have never done this themselves, they just might enjoy learning with their children.

Get your bunch in the wagon, on the wagon, or in any possible way to the water and wet your worms or plop your plugs. Super closeness possible! Proceed at virtually no risk at all...

Feeding Time: A simple and beautiful idea: save your bread crumbs and loaf-of-the-bread-heels, take the family to the park, and feed the goodies to ducks at the pond or to pigeons brave enough to come close. You might even lure some other bird to a little open pile of crumbs. Shades of Mary Poppins! Feed the birds...

Dad and Daughter / Mom and Son Night Out: Occasionally let Dad take any and all (together or at separate times) the daughters out to dinner at some place of their choice. Same with Mom: take the boys out (let them take you out) and spend some very good time together.

There is genuine value in each parent having this kind of time with each of the children with some forethought and planning. What usually happens is you find yourselves talking to each other...

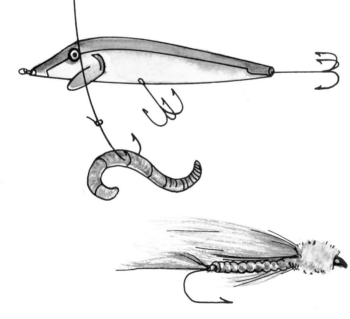

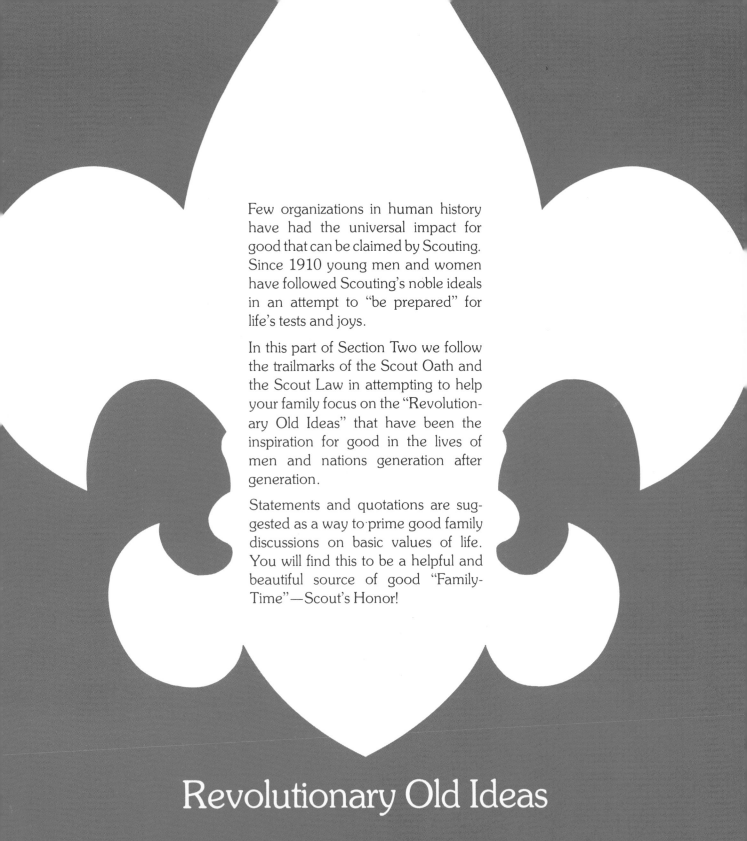

Few organizations in human history have had the universal impact for good that can be claimed by Scouting. Since 1910 young men and women have followed Scouting's noble ideals in an attempt to "be prepared" for life's tests and joys.

In this part of Section Two we follow the trailmarks of the Scout Oath and the Scout Law in attempting to help your family focus on the "Revolutionary Old Ideas" that have been the inspiration for good in the lives of men and nations generation after generation.

Statements and quotations are suggested as a way to prime good family discussions on basic values of life. You will find this to be a helpful and beautiful source of good "Family-Time"—Scout's Honor!

Revolutionary Old Ideas

"On my honor I will do my best to do my duty to God and my country and to obey the Scout Law; to help other people at all times; to keep myself physically strong, mentally awake, and morally straight."

On my honor: The stuff of integrity. To give your word and live up to it. To be counted on. A quality of life that makes you want to act the same way when no one is watching you as you do when you know you are being watched.

I will do my best: To summon up a maximum effort. To do all the good you know how to do. To do *not* what is just easy but what is right. To be self-motivated.

To do my duty to God ... To learn about and from God. To serve and love my fellow man. Not to be a demander. To realize what I *ought* to do. To take my religion seriously and practice in my daily life the qualities of life inherent in my understanding of the nature of God.

...and my country: To understand and obey the laws of my country. To be loyal to the government without being blind to possible flaws in the structures and persons in the nation's leadership. To do what my country has every right to expect of me.

To obey the Scout Law: The Scout Law declares the virtues and basic values of noble character. (Following these comments on the Scout Oath is a similar treatment of Scout Law.) The twelve points of the Scout Law are the "rules of the game."

To help other people at all times: Two great indicators of maturity are unselfishness and sensitivity to others. Helping others is a two-way street: the one receiving help is strengthened and relieved in his or her struggle; the one helping draws immense satisfaction from the "good deed" done.

To keep myself physically strong: To be aware of one's personal welfare. To resist every effort of environment and circumstance to make you weak and ineffectual. Not to pollute your body any more than you would a beautiful mountain stream. To be aware of all the forces at work to destroy your physical stamina; to resist drugs in every form.

Mentally awake: Good descriptive words: "alert," "sharp," or "bright." To pursue knowledge and wisdom. The desire to know. The capacity to notice. To be aware.

Morally straight: Developing into a person of character. Honest. Faithful to high ideals. Thoughtful of the rights of others. Truthful.

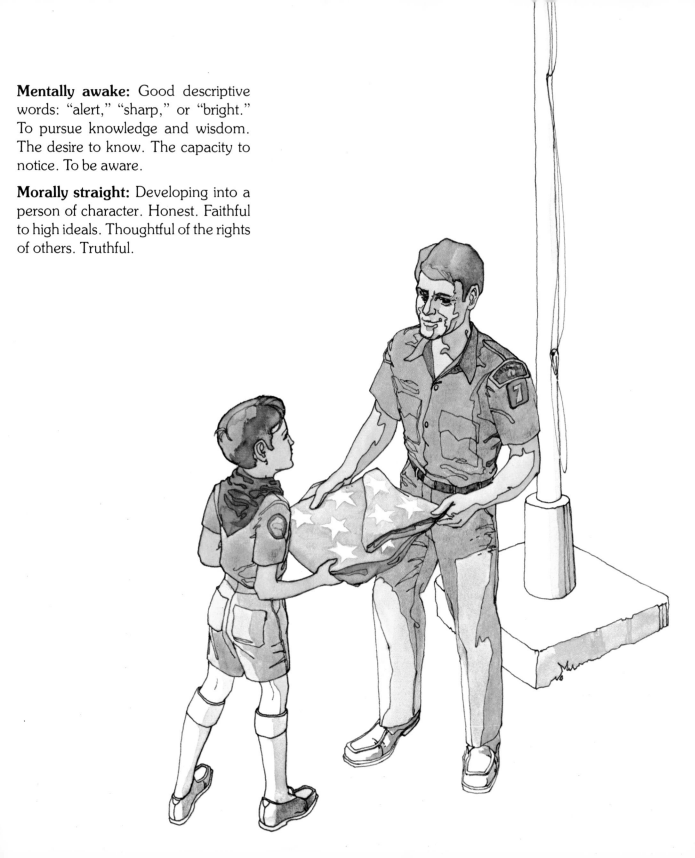

The Scout Law

"A Scout is trustworthy, loyal, helpful, friendly, courteous, kind, obedient, cheerful, thrifty, brave, clean and reverent."

Trustworthy—literally, to be worthy of trust. To tell the truth. You can be depended upon. Not cheating. Doing what you say you will do. *Discuss:*

a. "The best lightning-rod for your protection is your own spine." (Emerson)
b. "Try not to become a man of success but rather try to become a man of value." (Einstein)

Loyal—to be true to family, friends and nation. To be steadfast in commitments. To establish good priorities and live firmly by them. *Discuss:*

a. "A man who lacks reliability is utterly useless." (Confucius)
b. "Without consistency there is no moral strength." (John J. Owen)
c. "Learn to say 'no'; it will be of more use to you than to be able to read Latin." (Charles Haddon Spurgeon)

Helpful—to be concerned about others' welfare without thought of personal reward. "Do a good turn daily." To learn to look for needs; to be willing to respond to them. Unselfishness. *Discuss:*

a. "The way to be nothing is to do nothing." (Nathaniel Howe)
b. "Wherever there is a human being there is a chance for kindness." (Seneca)
c. "Help thy brother's boat across, and lo! thine own has reached the shore." (Hindu Proverb)
d. "Anyone can be polite to a king. It takes a gentleman to be polite to a beggar." (author unknown)

Friendly—a friend to all. A brother to others. To seek to understand others. To respect the customs and ideas of others. Thinking about the other person's feelings. To be genuinely interested in the other person. *Discuss:*

a. "We should ever conduct ourselves towards our enemy as if he were one day to be our friend." (John Henry Newman)
b. "I expect to pass through life but once. If therefore, there be any kindness I can show, or any good thing I can do to any fellow being, let me do it now, and not defer or neglect it, as I shall not pass this way again." (Penn)
c. "Blessed are they who have the gift of making friends, for it is one of God's best gifts. It involves many things, but above all, the

power of going out of one's self, and appreciating whatever is noble and loving in another." (Thomas Hughes)

Courteous—politeness, good manners. To act with consistent respect for others. Doing thoughtful things. Making life easier for others. *Discuss:*

a. "The greater man, the greater courtesy." (Alfred Lord Tennyson)
b. "Manners are rather to be learnt by example than rules." (John Locke)
c. "No one is useless in this world who lightens the burden of it to anyone else." (Charles Dickens)

Kind—the strength of gentleness. To treat others as you want to be treated. The attitude of care in all of nature. To treat all creatures and people with affection. *Discuss:*

a. "I have yet to find a man, whatever his situation in life, who did not do better work and put forth greater effort under a spirit of approval than he ever would do under a spirit of criticism."
(Charles M. Schwab)
b. "His life was gentle, and the elements so mixed in him that Nature might stand up and say to all the world: This was a man."
(Shakespeare)

c. "Throw away thy rod,
Throw away thy wrath;
Take the gentle path."
(George Herbert)

Obedient—to follow the rules. Conforming to the laws of the country, the limitations set by the family. Realizing that rules and laws are for our good and not just for our restriction. Taking proper steps to change rules that seem to be unfair or unjust. *Discuss:*

a. "The world no longer has a choice between force and law. If civilization is to survive it must choose the rule of law." (Dwight D. Eisenhower)
b. "There's too much talk about enforcing laws and not enough said about obeying them." (Arnold Glasow)
c. "Willing conformity to law gives man his finest freedom."(Richard L. Evans)

Cheerful—optimist, looking for the bright side of things. Happy to do the tasks that come your way, trying to make others happy. Joyful. Peaceful. *Discuss:*

a. "The secret of happiness is not in doing what one likes to do, but in liking what one has to do." (Sir James M. Barrie)

b. "If we have not peace within ourselves, it is vain to seek it from outside sources." (author unknown)
c. "I know what happiness is, for I have done good work." (Robert Louis Stevenson)
d. "A merry heart doeth good like a medicine; but a broken spirit drieth the bones." (Old Testament, Proverbs 17:22)

Thrifty—careful use of resources. Not wasteful—of time, money, other possessions. Careful planning for possible catastrophes. Taking good care of possessions. Good maintenance. *Discuss:*

a. "Never spend your money before you have it." (Thomas Jefferson)
b. "My father taught me that a bill is like a crying baby and has to be attended to at once." (Anne Morrow Lindbergh)
c. "If you want to earn more than you get, you need to be worth more than you are paid." (author unknown)
d. "When prosperity comes, do not use all of it." (author unknown)

Brave—handling danger even when afraid. The courage to stand for what is right even when you are the only one standing. Refusing to break rules. *Discuss:*

a. "Courage is grace under pressure." (E. Hemingway)
b. "No man is worth his salt who is not ready at all times to risk his body . . . to risk his well-being . . . to risk his life . . . in a great cause." (T. Roosevelt)
c. "Courage consists not in blindly overlooking danger, but in seeing and conquering it." (Jean Paul Richter)

Clean—keep the body and mind fit and in shape. To live with clean ideals. Helping keep the home, the community, the environment clean. Dealing with the "dirt" of life inside and outside. *Discuss:*

a. "Two ways to clean up a home: don't mess it up, and clean up the messes." (author unknown)
b. "Let it be observed, that slovenliness is no part of religion; that neither this, nor any text of Scripture condemns neatness of apparel. Certainly this is a duty, not a

sin. 'Cleanliness is, indeed, next to godliness.'" (John Wesley)

Reverent—proper regard for God, for the beliefs of others, for your own need to understand God more completely daily. Reverence is more than participation in religious services; it is living out in daily practice the deep truths of life that come from a clear understanding of the nature of God. *Discuss:*

a. "The best theology is rather a divine life than a divine knowledge." (Jeremy Taylor)

b. "Men will wrangle for religion; write for it; fight for it; die for it; anything but live for it." (Colton)

c. "Two men please God—who serves him with all his heart because he knows him; who seeks him with all his heart because he knows him not. (Panin)

d. "Anything that makes religion a second object makes it no object. He who offers to God a second place offers him no place." (Ruskin)

In addition to the profound insights from the pledges and laws of Scouting, there are numbers of other documents that have played critical parts in the development of human freedom and national strength. Listed below are several such documents. Shorter ones are listed in full; longer ones are mentioned with appropriate location sources. Check your local library, school or a bookstore for permanent copies.

You may wish to read and discuss any or all of them with your family. Certain selections lend themselves to oral reading on national holidays and religious festivals. These can help keep alive the deep roots of moral principle; share them from time to time with your family.

The Declaration of Independence (United States)

"WHEN in the Course of human Events, it becomes necessary for one People to dissolve the Political Bands which have connected them with another, and to assume among the Powers of the Earth, the separate and equal Station to which the Laws of Nature and of Nature's God entitle them, a decent Respect to the Opinions of Mankind requires that they should declare the causes which impel them to the Separation...."

**The Magna Carta
June 15, 1215;
February 11, 1225
Preamble (Great Britain)**

Check with your local library for a copy of the Magna Carta.

The Pledge of Allegiance (United States)

"I pledge allegiance to the flag of the United States of America, and to the republic for which it stands; one nation, under God, indivisible, with liberty and justice for all."

The Preamble to the United States Constitution

"We the People of the United States, in Order to form a more perfect Union, establish Justice, insure domestic Tranquility, provide for the common defense, promote the general Welfare and secure the blessings of liberty to ourselves and our posterity, do ordain and establish this Constitution for the United States of America."

The Ten Commandments

(The Old Testament, Exodus 20: 1-17)

The Golden Rule

"So whatever you wish that men would do to you, do so to them . . . ." (The New Testament, Matthew 7:12, RSV)

The Beatitudes

(The New Testament, Matthew 5: 1-11)

The Bill of Rights

(Amendments 1-10, The United States Constitution)

The Gettysburg Address (By Abraham Lincoln)

"Fourscore and seven years ago our fathers brought forth on this continent a new nation, conceived in liberty, and dedicated to the proposition that all men are created equal . . . ."

The Charter of The United Nations

"We the peoples of the United Nations determined to save succeeding generations from the scourge of war, which twice in our lifetime has brought untold sorrow to mankind, and . . . ."

69

Section Three

A special section of helps for parents
based on the awareness that no one is perfect
that all who try to "family" need
help, recommendations, understanding,
counsel, and an abundance of good fortune
to make it work.

*P*reface to Section Three: This section does not propose to be a condensed family life textbook. It is, rather, an effort to acknowledge that the best parents among us also have difficulties in raising their children. You will find here several brief ideas expanded ever so slightly to speak to common struggles among parents. The entire section is an effort to say, "If you are not altogether coping with the family task in A-plus fashion, welcome to the club!" You will find these topics discussed:

Between Parent and Parent—acknowledges that parents who don't make it well together have an extremely difficult time "doing family" very well.

The Teachable Moment—an encouragement to listen with the "third ear" and make full and helpful use of the opportunities your child will afford you to enhance your role as parent/teacher.

Where To Go For Help—for the time when you may be hurting, bewildered, needy. Here are some basic—very basic—suggestions that may start you on a successful search for the help you need most at the moment and through the long haul . . .

The Greater Family—a super idea! How to invent a family when you're away from your family. An idea dreamed up by a city-dweller who missed the "gathering of the clan" back home. Had a family in the neighborhood and didn't even know it . . .

Sex Education in the Family—encourages parents to do their "homework" on sex education; firmly asserts that parents *are*, whether or not they wish to be, the prime sex educators for their children.

Bibliography—excellent suggestions for books and other materials that can help your family.

Between Parent and Parent

The "lump of yeast" that gives rise to good family communication is the ferment provided by good parent-to-parent communication. The blind cannot lead the blind; so it is that parents who cannot (or do not) communicate well with one another cannot lead the family in good interaction. In short: if parents are going to do a superior job of creating and maintaining a healthy family spirit, they must determine to work at the fine art of sharing with one another well.

Two helpful words should be in the conscious vocabulary of every good parent: *openness* and *honesty*. If these concepts are absent parent-to-parent, you can be sure they will not be present parent-to-child.

Openness is essentially the willingness to grow, a distaste for ruts, eagerly standing on tip-toe for a better view of what tomorrow brings. A man once bought a new radio, brought it home, placed it on the refrigerator, plugged it in, tuned it to WSM in Nashville, Tennessee (home of the Grand Ole Opry), and then *pulled all the knobs off!* He had already tuned in all he ever wanted or expected to hear.

Some marriages are "rutted" and rather dreary because either or both partners have yielded to the tyranny of the inevitable, "what has been will still be." Stay open to newness. Stay open to change.

A popular movie carried the title: "If It's Tuesday, This Must Be Belgium!" Some families are like that: "If it's a Thursday, we'll be having meatloaf!" "If it's Monday, he'll wear the blue blazer." Don't "pull the knobs off." Stay alive to one another if you want to lead the family well.

Honesty is, quite plainly, truth-telling with love and compassion. Self expression and personal opinion are too frequently absent from too many families. The healthy couple will emphasize separate identities, individual interests, personal taste, uniqueness.

Kahlil Gibran has written a beautiful book entitled, *The Prophet.* In it he has a section on marriage which is one of the great thoughts of man on the subject. A paraphrase of the idea is this: marriage should not be thought of as two islands becoming one landmass; instead, he sees marriage at its best as two islands that remain separate and distinct whose shores are washed by the mutual waters of love!

That's poetry! That's insight! Two people who are definite individuals who choose to live and love together, who allow one another freedom for self-expression, who feel the need to make significant personal contributions to the relationship—those two people can be free to say what they really feel.

Possible pitfall: Marriage cannot be its healthiest if a couple spends its energy and time establishing a significant relationship based on differences! The paradox of the whole marriage experience is that the best possible relationship will occur between people who work at building their life together around their common interests and their mutual tastes.

A Couple Inventory Test

This is a valuable exercise for any couple of any age after any amount of time in marriage. Each person should make a list of the ten things he or she most loves to do in the whole world. (*Example:* she loves to go to the ballet and symphony; he loves baseball and bowling.) After making the list, have a heart-to-heart discussion about being willing to do with each other some of the things on the list. He may absolutely despise the symphony and she may loathe bowling; but "I'll symphony if you'll bowl" can be a powerful swap in family togetherness.

An honest relationship demands that people be willing to hear each other. Much conflict in marriage can be resolved with a willingness to try new things, experience new adventures.

Honesty also necessitates the willingness to share feelings that are very positive. Many couples lose a good thing with each other because one or both refuse to say, "You look great today," and think of honesty as the need to say, "How about something besides meatloaf next Thursday!"

No apologies for this statement whatsoever: *the family setting is the ideal place for proper sex education and proper attitudes regarding sex as a vital part of life.* It is a fact that the basic sexual attitudes of children are formed with and around their parents and brothers and sisters. The question is not: "Will I educate my child regarding sex?" It is rather: "How am I going about educating my child regarding sex?"

The healthiest families treat sex education as a very normal part of their lives together. Curiosity for the mind of a child is what hunger is for his stomach—it is a basic craving to know and to know more. It is critical in a child's development that he learn well and learn correctly.

Three suggestions: (1) Try to treat sexual curiosity with an attitude of "this is normal." Most adults who are seriously confused about their sexual attitudes trace their frustration to parents who were too cautious and guarded in this area.

(2) Work hard at laying a foundation of openness about sexuality. Encourage children to feel free to ask or say what is really on their minds . . . this may be the beautiful "teachable moment" occurring in your relationship to the child.

(3) Read good information about the family role in sexual preparation. Talk with your pediatrician or family doctor about special problems. Stay out in front of your children like the navigator on a ship or plane: know where you are headed, be confident of how to get there, consult your map often, and make a potentially difficult journey appear to be routine because you were so ready!

Sex Education in the Family

The Greater Family

The Time: Fifty years ago, Sunday afternoon, 3:30.
The Place: Farm home, front yard, under shade trees in a cool breeze.
The Participants: Grandparents, parents and children—cousins, nephews, nieces, uncles, aunts, step-children, a host of near and distant kin.
The Occasion: Just being together as usual.

You have just seen a brief description of a solemn and meaningful part of earlier life in the United States: the close proximity and frequent together-time of the greater family.

The greater family is essentially the close nucleus of grandparents, parents and children with the "larger ripples in the pond" of all the cousins and near-kin. Before children grew up, married and left for the cities, there was a charming closeness to most family life in this country. The massive congestion of urban sprawls has lifted small families out of places like Tupelo, Mississippi, and put them down lonely in cities like Toledo. Families that get together regularly are a rarity . . . and are generally blessed because of it.

Here is an exciting idea for today, taking into consideration the miles and clutter that fragment most families for their "cousins twice removed." It is a way to create your own "greater family" no matter where you live.

A minister moved from Kentucky to Washington, D.C. and lived in one of the many suburbs surrounding the city for four years. Soon after arriving, his family started to suffer from the isolation from their greater family members back home. He and his family finally hit on a grand notion and had genuine success with it. They "manufactured" their own greater family!

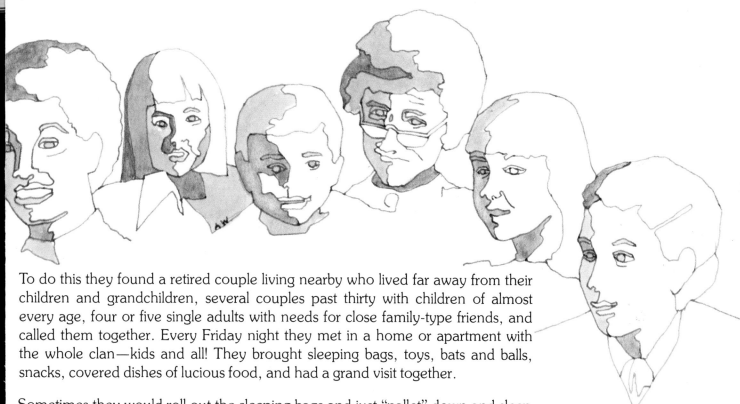

To do this they found a retired couple living nearby who lived far away from their children and grandchildren, several couples past thirty with children of almost every age, four or five single adults with needs for close family-type friends, and called them together. Every Friday night they met in a home or apartment with the whole clan—kids and all! They brought sleeping bags, toys, bats and balls, snacks, covered dishes of lucious food, and had a grand visit together.

Sometimes they would roll out the sleeping bags and just "pallet" down and sleep for the night. Sometimes they would show slides and movies of one another. Sometimes they'd make a bushel of popcorn. They had picnics, cookouts, laughter, and tears together. They became a family.

When you'd have a car problem, you never hesitated to ask a "family" member to go with you to leave your car for repairs and drive you home. When you had a chance to take your wife away for a weekend business/pleasure trip, you didn't think anything about asking one of the other "family" members to take care of the children so you could get away for a short trip.

The feeling of family turned the city into a friend instead of an enemy. The closeness brought tranquility to beleaguered parents and children. People belonged to people close to them.

What a great idea! This would be a nifty way to do some FamilyTimes together—with the greater family. You might want to try it with one or two couples and see how it grows. It just might be that the greater family could help your family be a greater family!

The Teachable Moment

Marvin, Jr. has just cut his foot. He is in tears. He screams. He sobs. He jumps up and down on the remaining foot. *Be assured:* this is not the ideal time to discuss with him his failure to practice the accordion.

Valerie has just come running in from school. She screams. She dances. She kick-jumps. She has just been elected cheerleader for the coming year. *Know this:* this is the wrong time to deal with her tendency to leave her bed unmade as she leaves for school each morning.

A child really hears you better if you weep when he weeps, cry when he cries, laugh when he laughs! Parents would do well to resist the temptation to *decide* when a child is ready to learn in favor of *discovering* the time when he or she is teachable.

The Greek language has two words for time: *chronos* and *kairos. Chronos* (pronounced *crow-noss*) is the root word for the English word *chronicle, chronology, chronograph.* It is the word used to measure time (as in hours, minutes, decades). *Kairos* (pronounced *kye-ross*) carries the meaning of appropriateness, ripeness, openness, season.

> *Chronos:* "It is 10:30 a.m."
> *Kairos:* "It is time to propose marriage."

Good family communication happens best in families where parents are sensitive to the *kairos* of teaching/learning. The best word for the *kairos* moment is the *teachable moment*, the moment when things are just right for correction, encouragement, affection, distance, questions or answers.

The tendency in most family relationships is to criticize at the moment of failure and to praise at the moment of success. The teachable moment for correction just might be in a quiet, riding-to-the-Little-League, late snack, totally off-guard un-threatening time. The teachable moment for affirmation just might be during tooth-brushing, homework, after mowing the lawn, totally off-guard, unthreatening time. Emphasis: *on totally off-guard, unthreatening time.*

A guiding principle for awareness of the teachable moment: *stay alert to curiosity in your child.* Listen to the big question behind the little question. A great time to teach is when a child asks, when he or she really wants to know.

It is the moment when your wisdom touches his need.
Traumas and tragedies are teachable moments.
Celebrations and holidays are teachable moments.
In the plainest language . . .
Stay alert to your children;
Answer questions as fully as possible;
Want to help; love to share.

Example: Your child runs in with a baby bird that has fallen out of a nest. When the bird is back in place with mom's and dad's help, a beautiful moment presents itself to talk about how parents love and care for their children. "Just like the mother bird will miss her baby and worry about their children when they are 'out of the nest.'" Good time to point up the reasons for checking in with parents periodically so they will not be unnecessarily concerned with the child's absence from the home.

Teachable moments come to you all the time. Be ready. Be available. You'll be helpful!

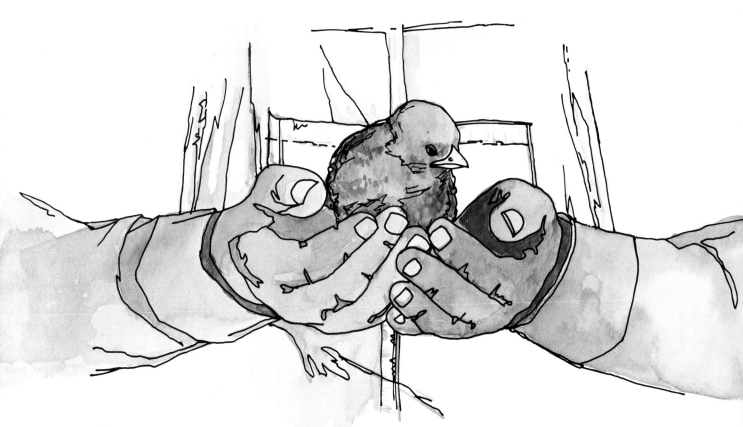

Where to go for Help

You are the victim of a sickness. You are in pain, discomfort and distress. You immediately seek the help of a competent physician who can prescribe the necessary treatment. You trust his opinion. You follow his advice.

You experience overwhelming financial setbacks, unanticipated. You are involved in enormous debt, anxiety, embarrassment. You seek the help of a banker, accountant or "knowledgeable brother-in-law" to help you sort out the tangles and "get the boat floating again."

You are part of a fractured family. Tension is high. Communication is low. The pace is either frantic or dragging along. You are hurting "all over more than anyone else." Where can you go for help? Several places...

But first, an encouraging word: multitudes of books, agencies, institutions, and other sources exist for the sole purpose of restoring meaning to family life for couples and families. The unbelievable fact is that *more help exists than people take advantage of.*

Let's look at several "helps" available:

One immediate source of help to families, and rightfully so, is the preferred church, synagogue or other religious order. You will frequently find ministers, rabbis, priests who have special training in dealing with family crises. Most of them will eagerly give time and attention to these problems. One crucial suggestion. A competent minister or other religious leader will readily refer you or your family member to more competent help if he or she does not feel adequately prepared to handle the situation.

Or try the Yellow Pages of your phone book. Look under *Family Service Organizations.* You should find listed there a number of agencies that can be helpful to you with whatever problem or problems you may be having. You may be in a small community and cannot locate such agencies in the Yellow Pages. If so, try this address:

> Family Service Association of America
> 192 Lexington Avenue
> New York, New York 10016

Write and ask for the names of agencies near you to assist you and your family with your particular need.

Your library is a superb resource for materials on family matters. Maybe you need a book or other materials on sharpening communication skills. Perhaps you need assistance with family problems. Ask the librarian to direct you to the proper center for such materials and dig in with gusto!

A local bookstore may have assorted aids for your family needs. There is an abundance of writing in the area of marriage and family matters today. Browse through them with healthy caution (as you should do your library!) with the awareness that a book is not authoritative just because it got printed! Much information sells for profit!

Much help is out there waiting. You will possibly feel awkward asking for assistance from place to place, but it is far better to feel awkward being taught to swim than to drown in a crisis because you didn't get courage enough to take lessons!

American Family Society. A new non-profit membership organization with the single aim of helping parents succeed in their challenging family responsibilities. Located in the Nation's Capital, the Society will draw on an abundance of information derived from sources that include the Library of Congress and many specialized libraries, subject matter experts, national organizations with programs that significantly relate to the quality of family life in America, and from successful parents throughout the Country. Members of the Society will receive monthly a full-color newsletter, *Family Matters*, packed with useful ideas on selected topics, and references for those who wish to dig for further information. For details, write:

> American Family Society
> Box 9873
> Washington, D.C. 20015

The Angry Book, Theodore Isaac Rubin, New York, Macmillan, 1969.   **Suggested Reading**

This is a neat book on expressing angry and very honest feelings in marriage. For couples where there is a need to talk it out instead of pouting or "swelling up over it," this could be a great spare tire in case you have one wearing thin and rough roads are expected. Getting it up and out and on the table could be one of the best experiences for any marriage.

Between Parent and Child, 1965
Between Parent and Teenager, 1969, Haim Ginott, Macmillan, New York.

Both books should be on the shelf for parents who are willing to grow with their children. You might do a good job of raising children without them; you'll do a better job with them . . .

Born to Win, Muriel James and Dorothy Jongeward, Addison-Wessley Publishing Co., Reading, Massachusetts, 1971.

This book is similar to *I'm OK; You're OK*—it is based on the techniques of transactional analysis. It is a bit easier to read and a little clearer to understand than *I'm OK; You're OK.* It should be very helpful in trying to understand the need to affirm one another in the family, to be able to look for the individual and personal strengths so necessary to family communication.

Confessions of a Workaholic, Wayne E. Oates, World Publishing Company, New York, 1971.

This is a delightful treatment of a frustrating subject: *how to cope with work addiction.* Oates is a minister/counselor/writer with a keen eye for the termites of anxiety that bore into the hard oak of family and personal life. Anyone with a compulsion to work (executive, mechanic, housewife, teacher) should read and will greatly benefit from practicing the helps of this fine book.

Free to Be. . . You and Me, conceived by Marlo Thomas, a project of the Ms Foundation, Inc., published by McGraw-Hill Book Co., New York, 1974.

Seldom has a book hit its target any better! *Free to Be. . . You and Me* is aimed at the little girl who should be opening her eyes to the wide world before her. It is aimed at the little boy who needs to learn to be sensitive and gentle instead of rough and tough. It is accompanied by an album of music and readings as well as a tape recording. You will love to hear Rosie Greer, former pro-football all star sing, "It's All Right to Cry." Children will love its message and benefit from it . . .

How to Father, Fitzhugh Dodson, Nash Publishing Company, Los Angeles, 1970.

This book is aimed at the father—married, widowed, divorced. It is an effort to amplify for men the charm and joy of rearing children. It has a marvelous appendix full of ideas like: "A Father's Guide to Toys;" "Equipment a Father Can Make;"

"A Father's Guide to Children's Books;" "A Survival Kit for Fathers." The appendix is fully one-fourth of the book. The work does not in any way play down the role of mother; it does acknowledge in a very healthy way the growing view that it takes the best efforts of *both* parents to make child-rearing work!

How to Parent, Fitzhugh Dodson, Nash Publishing Co., Los Angeles, 1974.

Dodson scores again in giving guidance to parents on child-rearing. A healthy, contemporary approach to the struggles and realities of parenthood. A super "mechanic's guide to the machinery of family!"

I'm OK; You're OK, Thomas Harris, Harper and Row, New York, 1969.

You will be into some pretty deep stuff in this book, but it is the classic popular treatment of a counseling and psychotherapeutic technique called "transactional analysis." The best way to condense the book is to re-read the title. It is intended to help you feel OK about yourself and about others; this would be a great basis for raising children and for dealing with people in everyday life. Expect it to be "heady" to get through, but well worth the journey.

"P.E.T." (Parent Effectiveness Training), Thomas Gordon, Published by Peter H. Wyden, Inc., 750 Third Avenue, New York, New York 10017.

This is a highly recommended book which is the source of a contemporary program dealing with the role of parent and how to anticipate and meet the various needs and situations that arise with children. This entire concept is remarkably well thought of across the spectrum of child-rearing experts.

Stress, Prepared by Blue Cross Association.

This is a small magazine-style book which deals with stress from several angles. It ranges from infancy to aging, stress situations that occur in home, at work, in the environment, and stress brought on by sudden changes. It includes one chapter on "the nervous breakdown," and a special article on "how to relax."

The book can be secured through your local Blue Cross. It is written primarily by physicians.

The Stork is Dead, Charlie Shedd, Word Publishing Co., Waco, Texas.

Quite simply put, the title tells it all. It is a super book on how to discuss matters of sex-information and sex-curiosity with your children. Some parents may even learn a bit about how and why they are put together as they are . . .

Shedd is a marvelous husband/father/grandfather who has done well with his own ideas and has raised a terrific family that loves each other.

Where Did I Come From?, Peter Mayle, Published by Lyle Stuart, Inc., 120 Enterprise Avenue, Secaucus, N.J. 07904.

This is a book written *for* parents but *to* children. The subtitle reads: "The facts of life without any nonsense and with illustrations." The book is done with chubby cartoon characters and is quite frank and explicit. Parents who wish to deal with the facts of life with no secrets and with cute candor will love the book. Excellent for showing small children where their expected baby brother or sister is coming from. This book may be the salvation of red-faced parents everywhere . . .

Widow, Lynn Caine, Published by William Morrow & Co., Inc., New York, 1974.

There are ten million women in our society who are widows; one out of every six women over twenty-one years of age in the United States is a widow. Lynn Caine is one of them.

This book is a moving account of her struggle to cope with life after the early and untimely death of her husband. It is practical. It is honest. It is timely. Every wife and mother can learn from her how best to approach the disaster that can befall any married woman. She has found the courage to share from her own pain.

The United States Jaycees' Family Life Program offers a structured program with books, learning guides, and local community discussion groups. Write:

> U.S. Jaycees Products Division
> Box 7
> Tulsa, Oklahoma 74102

National Geographic WORLD, a new periodical in full color for young readers ages 7 to 13. Order from:

> National Geographic Society
> 17th and M Streets
> Washington, D.C. 20036